NATIONAL GEOGRAPHIC KiDS

LOOK&LEARN

Dig

SCHOLASTIC INC.

It is fun to play in a sandbox!

You can dig in the sand with your hands or with a shovel.

Dogs like to play, too. This dog digs in the sand on a beach.

GUESS WHAT?

A dog digs with its front paws.

A mommy and daddy dig in the garden to plant flowers.

GUESS WHAT?

Food and water move up the roots to the flower.

flower

leaf

roots

A baby polar bear is born inside the cozy snow den.

GUESS WHAT?

A polar bear cub stays with its mother until the cub is two years old.

It leaves the den in the springtime.

A squirrel digs a hole to hide a nut.
It hides lots of nuts to eat later.

The hungry squirrel digs up the nuts it hid.
It digs through the snow to find them.

GUESS WHAT?

Nuts that stay buried grow to become trees.

**Look at all the diggers
you learned about.**

Who digs to play?

Who digs to plant flowers?

What digs a snow den?

What digs to hide food?

**What digs to make
a new building?**

ISBN 978-0-545-89954-3

Copyright © 2015 by National Geographic Society. All rights reserved.
Published by Scholastic Inc., 557 Broadway, New York, NY 10012, by arrangement with National Geographic Society.
SCHOLASTIC and associated logos are trademarks and/or registered trademarks of Scholastic Inc.

12 11 10 9 8 7 6   18 19 20/0

Printed in the U.S.A.   40

First Scholastic printing, November 2015

Text by National Geographic early childhood development specialist Catherine D. Hughes

DRMS: Dreamstime; SS: Shutterstock
Cover, Dmitry Kalinovsky/SS; 2–3, © Vladimir Popovic/istockphoto; 3 (LO), Zakaz/DRMS; 3 (UPRT), Petr Malyshev/DRMS; 4–5, Denis Babenko/DRMS; 6–7, © 237/Andrew Olney/Ocean/Corbis; 8–9, Filipe B. Varela/SS; 10–11, Amador García Sarduy/DRMS; 12–13, © Meinzahn/iStockphoto; 14–15, Design Pics/Richard Wear/Getty Images; 16–17, Eric Baccega/Nature Picture Library; 18–19, Elliotte Rusty Harold/SS; 20–21, Igor Teslavskiy/SS; 22 (UP), Design Pics/Richard Wear/Getty Images; 22 (LO), © Vladimir Popovic/istockphoto; 23 (UPLE), © 237/Andrew Olney/Ocean/Corbis; 23 (UPRT), Elliotte Rusty Harold/SS; 23 (LO), Amador García Sarduy/DRMS